The Little F Cooking from

Ideas for cooking with Early Years Foundation Stage children, using stories as starting points

Written by Sally Featherstone

Illustrations by Kerry Ingham

LITTLE BOOKS WITH BIG IDEAS

Published 2009 by A&C Black Publishers Limited
36 Soho Square, London W1D 3QY
www.acblack.com

First published 2002 by Featherstone Education Limited

ISBN 978-1-9041-8704-2

Text © Sally Featherstone 2002
Illustrations © Kerry Ingham 2007
Series Editor Sally Featherstone

A CIP record for this publication is available from the British Library.

Printed in Great Britain by Latimer Trend & Company Limited

This book is produced using paper that is made from wood grown in
managed, sustainable forests. It is natural, renewable and recyclable.
The logging and manufacturing processes conform to the environmental
regulations of the country of origin.

To see our full range of titles
visit **www.acblack.com**

Contents

Focus of the page		page number
Introduction		4–5
Encouraging Independence		6
Conversion Tables		8–9
The Three Bears	Porridge	10–11
The Enormous Pancake	American Pancakes	12–13
The Enormous Turnip	Vegetable Soup	14–15
The Gingerbread Man	Gingerbread Men	16–17
The Little Red Hen	Bread Rolls	18–19
The Very Hungry Caterpillar	Cup Cakes	20–21
Oliver's Milkshake	Bananas and Blueberry Milkshakes	22–23
Handa's Surprise	Fruit Sticks with Honey Yogurt	24–25
Pass the Jam, Jim	Easy Jam Whizzers and Jam Tarts	26–27
Pete's a Pizza	Mini Pizzas – Two Ways	28–29
Elmer the Patchwork Elephant	Painted Elephant Biscuits	30–31
Danny's Birthday	Birthday Cake	32–33
Making Faces	Expression Biscuits	34–35
Sally and the Limpet	Deep Sea Jellies	36–37
Having a Picnic	Currant Buns	38–39
The Little Boat	Sailing Boat Rolls	40–41
When the Teddy Bears Came	Honey Buns	42–43
Don't Forget the Bacon!	Bacon Sandwiches	44–45
Dogger	Chocolate Pennies	46–47
It's the Bear!	Baby Blueberry Muffins	48–49
Rosie's Walk	Popcorn Strings	50–51
Hello Beaky	Meringue Nests	52–53
Lights for Gita	Chapattis	54–55
The Last Noo-noo	Monster Cheese Biscuits	56–57
The Baked Bean Queen	Bean Dip	58–59
Meg and Mog	Pumpkin Soup	60–61
Oliver's Fruit Salad	Fruit Ice Lollies	62–63
Templates		64
Book List		65
More Conversions		66
Notes and Your Own Recipies		67

Introduction

The aim of this Little Book is to provide practitioners with ideas for cooking activities linked to well known and loved stories, traditional tales and stories with a multicultural element.

Cooking and stories are two essential elements of early learning. Together, they offer opportunities to experience all areas of learning and provide enjoyable activities to help children to make progress towards the Early Learning Goals.

Links with the Early Learning Goals for the Early Years Foundation Stage

Experiences of cooking and participating in storytelling offer the following opportunities:

Personal, Social and Emotional Development

- continue to be interested, excited and motivated to learn
- be confident to try new activities, initiate ideas and speak in a familiar group
- have a developing respect for their own cultures and beliefs, and those of other people
- work as part of a group or class, taking turns and sharing fairly, understanding that there need to be agreed values and codes of behaviour for groups of people, including adults and children, to work together harmoniously
- manage their own personal hygiene
- select and use activities and resources independently

Language, Communication and Literacy

- interact with others, negotiating plans and activities, and taking turns in conversations
- sustain attentive listening, responding to what they have heard by relevant comments, questions or actions
- listen with enjoyment and respond to stories, songs and other music, rhymes and poems
- use talk to organise, sequence and clarify thinking, ideas, feelings and events
- retell narratives in the correct sequence drawing on the language patterns of stories
- know that print carries meaning

- show an understanding of elements of stories, such as main character, sequence of events and how information can be found in non-fiction texts to answer questions about where, who, why and how
- attempt writing for various purposes, using features of different forms, such as lists, stories and instructions

Problem Solving, Reasoning and Numeracy

- say and use number names in order in familiar contexts
- count reliably up to ten everyday objects
- recognise numerals 1–9
- use developing mathematical ideas and methods to solve practical problems
- use language such as 'greater', 'smaller', 'heavier' or 'lighter' to compare quantities

Knowledge and Understanding of the World

- investigate objects and materials by using all of their senses
- find out about and identify some features of living things, objects and events they observe
- look closely at similarities, differences, patterns and change
- ask questions about why things happen and how things work
- select tools and techniques they need to shape, assemble and join the materials they are using

Physical Development

- recognise the importance of keeping healthy and things that contribute to this
- use a range of small and large equipment
- handle tools, objects, construction and malleable materials safely and with increasing control

Physical Development

- explore colour, texture, shape, form and space in two and three dimensions
- use their imagination in art and design, music, dance, imaginative role play and stories
- respond in a variety of ways to what they see, hear, smell, touch and feel
- express and communicate their ideas, thoughts and feelings by using designing and making

Every activity in this book meets a range of goals for learning. They are listed on each page.

Encouraging Independence

The activities in 'The Little Book of Cooking from Stories' are intended for children to complete with some help from adults. Younger children or those with special needs will need more support, but we would encourage you to let them do as much as they can themselves.

Even the youngest children can:

▶ prepare and organise their own work area

▶ mix, measure, crack and separate eggs, chop vegetables, spread butter and jam, scoop mixture, ice and decorate

▶ sort and organise decorations and materials

▶ choose the materials and equipment for their own work

▶ decide on the colours and patterns they will use

▶ choose who to work with

▶ write their own messages, cards and letters in 'have a go' writing, make labels and name and label their own work

▶ cut and tie string, and display their work

▶ help to clear up and put away equipment.

You can help young children by:

▶ encouraging them by asking helpful questions

▶ using opportunities to introduce new words and ideas

▶ listening to what they say

▶ observing how they work

▶ demonstrating tricky bits and finished processes

▶ handling the hot or complicated bits!

Some of the recipes in this book use eggs:
Safety Advice on Using Eggs

The advice to schools and settings is to use pasteurised eggs (either whole or separated) now available in supermarkets. Hard boiled eggs are quite safe for children to eat and to use in any recipe using cooked eggs.

Conversion Tables

The recipes in this book are in a mixture of measurement types. Some are in cups, some in spoons, and some in metric measures. It is important for children to realise early that measurements come in a range of types.

Here are conversion tables so you know how to convert a measurement if you don't have the right measuring utensils.

NB: Don't mix different sorts of measures in the same recipe!

Ounces and grams

Ounces	grams
1oz	28g
2oz	57g
3oz	85g
4oz	114g
5oz	142g
6oz	170g
7oz	175g
8oz	203g
9oz	227g
10oz	255g
16oz/1lb	454g
2lb	907g

Cups and millilitres (use the same cup each time!)

1 cup	250ml
half a cup	125ml
third of a cup	80ml
quarter of a cup	60ml

Level tablespoons in grams

1 tablespoon of rice	15g
1 tablespoon of sugar	15g
1 tablespoon of butter/margarine	15g
1 tablespoon of flour (not sifted)	8g
1 tablespoon of Parmesan cheese	5g
1 tablespoon of breadcrumbs	3–4g

Spoons and millilitres

tablespoon	15ml
1 teaspoon	5ml
half a teaspoon	2.5ml
quarter of a teaspoon	1.25ml

NB: Different recipe books give slightly different tables. We have gone with the majority view.

Fluid ounces and tablespoons

8 fluid ounces	16 tablespoons
4 fluid ounces	8 tablespoons
3 fluid ounces	5 tablespoons
2 fluid ounces	4 tablespoons

Cups and grams

1 cup of sugar	200g
1 cup of sifted flour	115g
1 cup of flour spooned from the bag	120g/4oz
1 cup of flour dredged from the bag	140g

Oven temperatures

Gas mark	Centigrade	Fahrenheit
1/4	110°C	225°F
1/2	130°C	250°F
1	140°C	275°F
2	150°C	300°F
3	160°C	325°F
4	180°C	350°F
5	190°C	375°F
6	200°C	400°F
7	220°C	425°F
8	230°C	450°F

At the end of the book, we have added a new conversion chart which enables you to convert recipes into cups, grams or ounces (remember not to mix them in the same recipe).

Story: The Three Bears

Recipe: Porridge
Make porridge for a winter snack and eat it with honey.

What you need for porridge for 4 or 5:

Ingredients

- 2 cups of water
- 1 cup of rolled porridge oats (not the 'quick' variety)
- milk
- honey or brown sugar
- sultanas or fresh fruit (optional)

Equipment

- a microwaveable bowl or a small saucepan
- a wooden spoon
- a bowl for each child
- spoons
- knife and board to cut up fruit (optional)

What you do

Saucepan method
1. Put the water and porridge in the saucepan.
2. Put the pan on the stove.
3. Heat on full power, stirring all the time, until the mixture boils.
4. Lower the heat and simmer for about 4 minutes until thick.
5. Spoon into the bowls.
6. Top with milk and sugar or honey.
7. Sprinkle some fresh fruit or sultanas on the top.

Microwave method
1. Mix the oats and water.
2. Put in a microwaveable bowl (no lid!).
3. Microwave on high for 1 minute.
4. Remove and stir well.
5. Cook again for 1 minute.
6. Spoon into the bowls.
7. Top with milk and sugar or honey.
8. Sprinkle some fresh fruit or sultanas on the top.
* Don't forget to talk about how the porridge oats look and feel before and after cooking.
** This mixture gets very hot – be careful and stir well before eating!

Other activities
▶ Turn your home corner into the Three Bears house or café.
▶ Use porridge oats to make flapjack.
  Mix 350grams of oats with 150grams of brown sugar, 175grams of melted butter or margarine and 1 tablespoon golden syrup. Press into a baking tray and bake at 190°C (375°F) for 25 minutes.

Early Learning Goals

PSD Select and use activities and resources independently.

LCC Listen with enjoyment and respond to stories, songs and other music, rhymes and poems.

PSRN Say and use number names in order in familiar contexts. Use language such as 'greater', 'smaller', 'heavier' or 'lighter' to compare quantities.

CR Use their imagination in imaginative role play and stories.

Story: The Enormous Pancake

Recipe: American Pancakes

These little pancakes are easy to make and fun to eat. Read the book as you eat the pancakes!

What you need for 20 small pancakes:

I will need

Ingredients

- ▶ 350g (12oz) plain flour
- ▶ 1 teaspoon of salt
- ▶ 2 tablespoons of sugar
- ▶ 2 teaspoons of baking powder
- ▶ 2 eggs
- ▶ 300–350ml (10–12 fl oz) milk
- ▶ 3 tablespoons of melted butter or oil, plus some for oiling the pan

Safety Advice on Using Eggs (page 7)

Equipment

- ▶ a teaspoon
- ▶ a tablespoon
- ▶ a big bowl
- ▶ a small bowl
- ▶ a sieve
- ▶ a whisk or beater
- ▶ a cup to break eggs into
- ▶ a small frying pan
- ▶ a spatula
- ▶ plates for the pancakes
- ▶ a clean squeezy bottle if you want to make scribble pancakes

What you do

1. Sift the flour, baking powder, salt and sugar into the bowl.
2. Make a well in the centre with a spoon.
3. Help the children to break the eggs into a cup. Add the milk.
4. Pour this mixture into the flour mixture.
5. Mix everything together.
6. Add the melted butter or oil.
7. If the mixture is very thick, add a bit more milk.
8. Cover the bowl and set aside while you heat the pan.
9. Lightly grease the pan with the butter or oil and heat it.
   (It is hot enough when water dropped on the surface bounces about.)
10. Pour 2 tablespoons of batter into the pan and cook for 1–2 minutes, until bubbles break on the surface.
11. Turn the pancake with the spatula and cook the other side.
12. When they are cooked, lift the pancakes onto a warm plate.
13. Eat with honey, jam or maple syrup.

Make some 'scribble' pancakes

*   Put some pancake mixture into a clean squeezy bottle.

**   Squeeze patterns or faces into the pan and leave for a few seconds before you gently pour the rest of the mixture over. Finish as before.

Other activities

▶ Make zigzag books of the story.
▶ Sequence the story with toy animals. Use the sand tray or a play mat and make a 'river' to cross.
▶ Make masks and play out the story.
▶ Turn your home corner into a pancake house or café.

Early Learning Goals

PSD	Be confident to try new activities, initiate ideas, work as part of a group taking turns and sharing.	Attempt writing for various purposes.
LCC	Use talk to organise, sequence and clarify thinking, ideas and events.	**K&U** Investigate objects and materials by using all of their senses. Look closely at change.
		PH Handle tools.

Story: The Enormous Turnip

Recipe: Vegetable Soup

This recipe gives children an opportunity to chop and cut for a real purpose. The story reminds the children how vegetables grow and of the importance of teamwork – even the smallest member of a group can make a contribution!

What you need for vegetable soup:

Ingredients

▶ a selection of vegetables – try carrots, onions, leeks, potatoes, parsnips, mushrooms, sweet potatoes, cabbage, peppers and turnips

▶ a tablespoon of oil

▶ 150ml water

▶ a vegetable stock cube

▶ salt and pepper

▶ herbs (optional)

▶ bread

▶ you can add tinned beans or tomatoes if you like

Equipment

▶ chopping boards

▶ knives (old table knives or school meal knives are not too sharp)

▶ a wooden spoon

▶ a big pan

▶ spoons and bowls

What you do

Children can do most of this recipe themselves if you let them. They need supervision but, in small groups, children are unlikely to hurt themselves if you cut the vegetables into big pieces with a flat side first. If you feel concerned, let them watch and talk about the process while you do it.

1. Talk about the vegetables as the children wash them.
2. Cut the vegetables into big chunks (you only need to peel sweet potatoes and onions).
3. Get the children to cut the vegetables into small pieces (or talk to them whilst you cut the vegetables).
4. Heat the oil in the pan and fry the onion pieces briefly.
5. Add all the other vegetables, the stock cube and the water (and the tomatoes if used).
6. Simmer until the vegetables are tender. Stir from time to time and add more water if needed.
7. Add the beans (if used) and reheat.
8. Spoon into the bowls.
9. Eat with bread.

Talk about the smells, colours and flavours before, during and after cooking.

** If you have any soup left over, put it in a liquidiser and make it into smooth soup. Talk about what happens as they watch the mixture whizz round.

Other activities

▶ Have a vegetable shop or a market stall outside.
▶ Use some vegetables to make prints.
▶ Read 'Oliver's Vegetables'.
▶ Plant some vegetables in your garden or in growbags or window boxes.
▶ Visit a market or vegetable shop.
▶ Look at/try unusual vegetables.

Early Learning Goals

PSD Select and use activities and resources independently.

K&U Investigate objects and materials by using all of their senses.
Find out about, and identify some features of objects they observe.

PH Use a range of small and large equipment.
Handle tools.

CR Respond in a variety of ways to what they see, hear, smell, touch and feel.

Story: The Gingerbread Man

Recipe: Gingerbread Men

Make your own gingerbread men to nibble as you tell the story. You could make all the story characters with gingerbread or salt dough to tell the story again.

What you need for 3 dozen gingerbread men (depending on the size of your cutters):

I will need

Ingredients

- ½ cup of butter/margarine
- ¾ cup of brown sugar
- 2 eggs
- ¾ cup of molasses or black treacle
- 4 ½ cups of plain flour
- 1¼ teaspoons of baking powder
- 1 tablespoon of cinnamon
- 2 teaspoons of ground ginger
- 1 teaspoon of mixed spice
- icing to decorate

Equipment

- scales or cup measures
- 2 large mixing bowls
- a wooden spoon
- a cup for the eggs
- boards and rolling pins
- cutters
- a spatula or slice
- baking sheets and a wire rack

What you do

1. In the large bowl, get the children to cream the butter/ margarine and the sugar until it looks light and fluffy.
2. Break the eggs one at a time into the cup and add to the mixture.
3. Beat well after adding each egg.
4. Add the molasses or black treacle.
5. Mix the rest of the ingredients together in the other bowl.
6. Spoon into the egg mixture, mixing well after each spoonful. They may need help as the mixture gets thicker.
7. Finish mixing the dough with your hands.
8. Wrap the dough in cling film and chill for an hour or two in a fridge or a cold place.
9. When the dough has chilled, heat the oven to 180°C (350°F), gas mark 4.
10. Break off pieces of dough and roll out on a floured board or clean table top to 5mm thickness.
11. Cut out gingerbread figures and lift with the slice onto lightly greased baking trays. (Make holes in the top with a straw if you want to hang the figures up.)
12. Cook for 10 to 15 minutes, depending on size.
13. Transfer to a wire rack.
14. When cool, use icing to make faces, buttons etc.

Other activities

▶ Act out the story – use long pieces of fabric or playground chalk to make roads and a river.
▶ Use small world people and animals to retell and sequence the story.
▶ Make some play dough and use with animal cutters and the gingerbread people cutters.

Early Learning Goals

LCC	Listen with enjoyment and respond to stories, songs, rhymes and poems. Use talk to sequence thinking and events. Show an understanding of elements of stories, such as main character and sequence.	K&U	Investigate materials by using all their senses.
		PH	Handle malleable materials with increasing control.
		CR	Explore texture, shape and form in three dimensions.

Story: The Little Red Hen

Recipe: Bread Rolls

Help the children to learn about growth and farming while they bake. This story also gives you an opportunity to talk about teamwork.

What you need for 16 small rolls:

Ingredients

▶ 1kg (2lb) white bread flour or half white flour and half wholemeal flour

▶ 2 teaspoons of salt

▶ 2 sachets of easy blend dried yeast

▶ 2 tablespoons of vegetable oil

▶ 550–600ml (18–20 fl oz) lukewarm water

▶ extra flour and oil for dusting and brushing

Equipment

▶ a large mixing bowl

▶ a sieve

▶ a tablespoon and a teaspoon

▶ a wooden spoon

▶ cling film

▶ a measuring jug

▶ scales

▶ a pastry brush and scissors

▶ baking trays and a wire rack

See page 66 for converting fluid oz. to ml.

What you do

1. Weigh the flour(s) and sieve them into the large bowl.
2. Add the salt and dried yeast, spoon in the oil and add the water.
3. Mix the oil and water into the flour with the wooden spoon until the dough is soft but not sticky. If it is too wet, add some more flour; if it is too dry, add a bit more water.
4. Turn the dough onto a board or a clean work surface.
5. Knead by pulling and rolling the dough backwards and forwards.
6. Keep kneading for 8 to 10 minutes until the dough is smooth and springy.
7. Put back in the mixing bowl and cover with an oiled piece of cling film.
8. Leave the dough in a warm place for at least an hour until it has doubled in size and feels spongy. (The cling film allows you and the children to see what is happening!)
9. Tip the dough out on the board and knead for a minute or two.
10. Cut the dough into 16 pieces to make:
    ▶ cottage rolls. Make a small ball and a bigger ball. Put the small ball on top and push the handle of a spoon through both.
    ▶ hedgehog rolls. Make a hedgehog shape and snip the surface with scissors to make the prickles. Add currants for eyes.
11. Cover the rolls and leave to double in size again.
12. Bake for 12 to 15 mins at 200ºC (400ºF) gas mark 6.

Other activities

▶ Make salt dough bread and cakes for a baker's shop.
▶ Get some wheat grains and grow them in a tray on the window-sill.
▶ Try grinding your own corn into flour in a pestle and mortar.
▶ Visit a windmill.
▶ Use puppets to retell the story.

Early Learning Goals

PSD	Work as part of a group or class.	**K&U**	Investigate objects and materials by using all of their senses. Look closely at change. Ask questions about why things happen.
LCC	Retell narratives in the correct sequence, drawing on language patterns of stories.		
PSRN	Use language such as 'heavier' or 'lighter'.	**CR**	Explore texture, shape and form in three dimensions.

Story: The Very Hungry Caterpillar

Recipe: Cup Cakes

This story is a favourite in all settings, for all ages, and gives many learning opportunities, particularly in language and maths.

What you need for 24 cup cakes:

Ingredients

▶ 125g butter or margarine

▶ 1 ¾ teaspoons of vanilla flavouring

▶ ½ cup of castor sugar

▶ 2 eggs

▶ 1 ½ cups of self-raising flour

▶ ½ cup of milk

▶ paper cake cases

▶ icing

▶ cherries, chocolate drops, sprinkles etc. to decorate

Safety Advice on Using Eggs (page 7)

Equipment

▶ a large mixing bowl

▶ a sieve

▶ a teaspoon

▶ a tablespoon

▶ a wooden spoon

▶ a measuring cup

▶ a cup to break eggs into

▶ bun or patty tins

▶ a wire cooling rack

▶ small knives for spreading icing (butter knives are perfect)

What you do

1. Heat the oven to 180°C (350°F), gas mark 4.
2. Put the butter/margarine and the sugar in the bowl and beat with the wooden spoon until pale and creamy.
3. Break the eggs one at a time and add them to the butter mixture, beating after you add each egg.
4. Sift in half the flour and stir in gently.
5. Sift in the other half of the flour and stir in gently.
6. Add the milk and stir again.
7. Put the paper cases in the patty tins.
8. Spoon the mixture into the cases.
9. Bake for about 15 minutes until lightly browned.
10. Remove from the oven and leave to cool on a wire rack.
11. Ice and decorate your cup cakes with whatever you have available. Encourage the children to be inventive!

* You can make butter icing with 30grams of butter, 2 cups icing sugar and 2 tablespoons of milk. Mix together and add food colouring of your choice.

* Make coloured coconut sprinkles by putting some dessicated coconut into small ziplock bags and adding a few drops of food colouring to each. Do up the zip and shake and rub it until the coconut is evenly coloured. Children love doing this!

Other activities

▶ Make some picture cards of the things the caterpillar ate. Sequence and count them.

▶ Make salt dough food and have a caterpillar food shop.

▶ Look for caterpillars in the garden.

▶ Make butterfly prints and patterns.

▶ Move like caterpillars and butterflies.

Early Learning Goals

PSD	Select and use activities and resources independently.	**PH**	Use a range of small and large equipment.
PSRN	Count and use language such as 'heavier' or 'lighter'.	**CR**	Explore colour, texture and shape in two and three dimensions.
K&U	Investigate objects and materials by using all their senses.		Express and communicate their ideas, thoughts and feelings by using designing and making.

Story: Oliver's Milkshake

Recipe: Banana and Blueberry Milkshakes

Where does the milk come from? This story explains in a humorous way. One of a series of food-related stories.

What you need for 6 small milkshakes:

Ingredients

▶ 2 ripe bananas

▶ half a punnet of blueberries (optional)

▶ 600ml (a pint) milk

Equipment

▶ a liquidiser or blender

▶ a knife

▶ small glasses or beakers

▶ straws

What you do

Children can do all the stages of this except the blender.

1. Wash and drain the blueberries.
2. Peel and chop the bananas.
3. Put the fruit and milk into the blender.
4. Blend for about a minute.
5. Pour into glasses or beakers and add a straw.

Some alternatives

* You can add almost any fruit to milkshakes.
  Try strawberries, mangoes, cherries (stoned), plums and raspberries. You could go shopping with the children, choose some fruit and then offer a range of choices.

* For a special occasion, add some ice cream. You will need to reduce the amount of milk to half a pint and add half a pint of ice cream for 4 milkshakes.

Other activities

▶ Make different flavours of milkshakes.

▶ Collect pictures of milk and milk products.

▶ Make butter by shaking milk in a screw-topped jar.

▶ Use farm animals to retell the story.

Early Learning Goals

PSD Be confident to try new activities. Select and use activities and resources.

LCC Use talk to organise, sequence and clarify thinking.

K&U Investigate objects and materials using all of their senses.

Find out about and identify some features of objects and events they observe.
Look at change.

PH Handle tools with control.

CR Respond to what they see, hear, smell, touch and feel.

Story: Handa's Surprise

Recipe: Fruit Sticks with Honey Yogurt

Handa had so many different fruits in her basket. Buy some and have a different sort of snack time.

What you need for 6 to 8 children:

Ingredients

- ▶ 220g (8oz) plain or flavoured yogurt
- ▶ 1 tablespoon of honey
- ▶ a pinch of cinnamon
- ▶ a range of fruits (bananas, strawberries, kiwi fruits, mangoes, pineapples, guavas, oranges and tangerines)

Equipment

- ▶ chopping boards
- ▶ knives (not too sharp!)
- ▶ peelers
- ▶ a big plate
- ▶ a bowl for the yogurt
- ▶ cocktail sticks

What you do

Talk about the fruit before you start. Feel the skins, smell the fruit, talk about where and how each fruit grows and how it gets to the shop or market.

1. Make the honey yogurt by mixing the honey and spice into the yogurt.
   * Prepare the fruit just before you want to eat it.
2. Wash all the fruit before you start (even the ones you are going to peel).
3. Peel mangoes, bananas, pineapples and any other fruit with skins.
4. Chop the fruit into bite-sized pieces.
5. Put the yogurt bowl in the middle of the plate and arrange the fruit round it.
6. Put some cocktail sticks in an egg cup or small glass.
7. Use the sticks to spear the pieces of fruit and dip them in the yogurt.

* This is a great exercise in fine motor control.
* Try this method with vegetable chunks and plain yogurt with chives or other herbs in it.

Other activities

▶ Go shopping for exotic fruit.
▶ Talk about healthy eating.
▶ Make a graph or chart of favourite fruits.
▶ Do fruit printing.
▶ Plant fruit pips and seeds.
▶ Plant an apple or pear tree in a tub in the garden.

Early Learning Goals

PSD	Select and use activities and resources independently.	PH	Handle tools, objects and materials safely and with increasing control.
PSRN	Use language such as 'heavier' or 'lighter' to compare.	CR	Explore colour, texture, shape and form in three dimensions.
K&U	Investigate objects and materials by using all their senses.		Respond in a variety of ways to smell, touch and feel.

Story: Pass the Jam, Jim

Recipe: Easy Jam Whizzers and Jam Tarts

Enjoy this rhyming book, then use some jam in cooking. These recipes use ready-made pastry, but you could make your own.

What you need for about 12 Jam Whizzers:

Ingredients

▶ 1 packet of ready-made puff pastry

▶ red jam (strawberry, raspberry or plum)

or 16 Jam Tarts:

Ingredients

▶ 1 packet of ready-made shortcrust pastry

▶ red jam (strawberry, raspberry or plum)

Equipment (for either recipe)

▶ boards or a clean work surface

▶ rolling pins

▶ a sharp knife (for adult use only)

▶ a tablespoon and a teaspoon

▶ cling film

▶ cutters for tarts

▶ baking trays (for Whizzers)

▶ Jam Tart tins (for Jam Tarts)

▶ a wire cooling rack

What you do

Jam Whizzers:

1. Unroll the pastry onto a board and roll out thinly into a rectangle.
2. Spread jam all over the pastry, leaving a gap round the edge.
3. Roll the pastry up into a tight roll (starting at the short side).
4. Wrap the roll in cling film and put in the fridge or a cold place for at least half an hour.
5. Turn the oven on to 200°C (400°F), gas mark 6.
6. Take the roll from the fridge and cut into slices about 2cm wide.
7. Put the whizzers on a baking tray and cook for 15 minutes until golden.
8. Cool on a wire rack.

Jam Tarts:

1. Unroll the pastry onto a board and roll out thinly.
2. Cut out circles and put them in jam tart tins. Gather up the left-over bits and roll out again to cut more circles.
3. Spoon some jam into each tart.
4. Bake at 200°C (400°F), gas mark 6 for 15 minutes until the pastry is brown. Cool on a wire rack.

** Jam gets very hot when cooking. Cool thoroughly before eating!

Other activities

▶ Make some salt dough jam tarts and use for counting or shopping.
▶ Make some jam or marmalade using a microwave recipe.
▶ Play rhyming games with children's names.
▶ Make jam sandwiches and have a party or a picnic outside.

Early Learning Goals

PSD Select and use activities and resources independently.

LCC Use talk to organise, sequence and clarify thinking and events. Retell narratives in the correct sequence.

PSRN Say and use number names in order in familiar contexts.

Count reliably to ten objects.

K&U Investigate materials by using all of their senses.

PH Use a range of small and large equipment.
Handle tools and malleable materials.

Story: Pete's a Pizza

Recipe: Mini Pizzas – Two Ways

This quirky book is about a boy and his father's game to cheer him up on a rainy day. Make some pizza snacks to cheer up your children!

What you need for pizza snack breads:

I will need

Ingredients

▶ half a hamburger bun for each child
▶ melted butter
▶ ham slices (optional)
▶ cheese slices
▶ dried mixed herbs or oregano

or Mini Pizzas:
Ingredients

▶ bread recipe from page 17, made to step 10
▶ a can of chopped tomatoes

▶ cheese slices
▶ sliced pepper, olives, sliced mushrooms and cherry tomatoes to decorate

Equipment (for either recipe)

▶ spoons and a knife
▶ a slice or spatula
▶ a wire cooling rack
▶ baking sheets
▶ a board and rolling pin

What you do

Pizza Snack Breads:

1. Slice the hamburger buns in half, brush with melted butter and brown lightly under a grill.
2. Cover each bun with a slice of ham (if used) and a slice of cheese.
3. Sprinkle with herbs and brown again under the grill until the cheese is bubbling.

** Cheese gets very hot when cooking. Make sure the pizzas have cooled down a bit before eating them!

Mini Pizzas:

1. Make the dough to step 10. Divide into 16 pieces.
2. Roll out each piece on a lightly floured board.
3. Place on a baking sheet and spread with chopped tomatoes.
4. Decorate with other vegetable pieces (encourage them to do their own and be inventive).
5. Bake for 10 minutes at 200°C (400°F), gas mark 6.
6. Lift onto plates with the spatula.

** Make sure the pizzas have cooled down before eating!

Other activities

▶ Turn your role play into a pizza delivery service.
▶ Write pizza recipes.
▶ Visit a pizza place or order a take-away delivery.
▶ Take photos of the way to make pizzas and turn them into a sequencing game.

Early Learning Goals

LCC	Use talk to organise, sequence and clarify events.	Look closely at differences and change.
PSRN	Say and use number names in order in familiar contexts.	**CR** Explore colour, texture and shape in two and three dimensions.
K&U	Investigate objects and materials by using all of their senses.	Express their ideas, thoughts and feelings by using designing and making.

Story: Elmer the Patchwork Elephant

Recipe: Painted Elephant Biscuits

Elmer is already a favourite character with most children. Make some Elmer biscuits and then decorate them.

What you need for about 30 biscuits:

I will need

Ingredients

- ▶ 110g (4oz) butter or margarine
- ▶ 110g (4oz) soft brown sugar
- ▶ 1 egg
- ▶ 225g (8oz) plain flour
- ▶ 1 pinch of salt
- ▶ 1 teaspoon of mixed spice

For decorating

- ▶ food colouring
- ▶ cotton buds

> **Safety Advice on Using Eggs**
> (page 7)

Equipment

- ▶ a large mixing bowl
- ▶ a sieve
- ▶ a teaspoon
- ▶ a tablespoon
- ▶ a wooden spoon
- ▶ an elephant cutter or card template
- ▶ boards and rolling pins
- ▶ a cup to break the egg into
- ▶ scales
- ▶ baking trays a and wire rack

What you do

1. Preheat the oven to 190°C (375°F), gas mark 5.
2. Mix the butter and sugar in the bowl until smooth and creamy.
3. Crack the egg into the cup and then add it to the mixture in the bowl.
4. Stir well.
5. Sift in the flour, salt and mixed spice, and mix to form a dough.
6. Sprinkle some flour on a board or clean work surface.
7. Take some of the dough and roll it out until about 5mm thick. (Don't roll too thin.)
8. Cut out elephant shapes and lift carefully onto the baking trays.
9. Bake for about 15 minutes until golden brown.
10. Cool on a wire tray.

Decorating the biscuits

You can either:

11. Mix some colouring with a very little water in some egg cups or small bowls.
12. Use the cotton buds to paint decorations on the biscuits.
    (Don't let the biscuits get too wet or they will disintegrate!)

Or:

Decorate with icing, sprinkles etc.

Other activities

▶ Make Elmer's jungle in the sand tray or brick play area.
▶ Offer some squared paper to make Elmer patterns with paint or crayons.
▶ Make collaborative patchwork pictures by sticking squares of coloured tissue paper on windows or sheets of white card with paste.

Early Learning Goals

PSD	Work as part of a group, taking turns and sharing fairly.	**K&U**	Select tools and techniques to shape materials.
LCC	Use talk to organise, sequence and clarify thinking, ideas, feelings and events.	**PH**	Use a range of small and large equipment. Handle tools and malleable materials safely and with increasing control.
PSRN	Say and use number names in order in familiar contexts.		

Story: Danny's Birthday

Recipe: Birthday Cake

Danny has a puzzle to solve when he mixes up the gift tags from his birthday presents. The cake gives a good opportunity to explore balance.

What you need for 1 cake:
Ingredients

- 4 eggs (size 3)
- 4oz butter or margarine
- 4oz sugar
- 4oz self-raising flour
- 1 teaspoon of vanilla flavouring

For the icing

- 225g (8oz) icing sugar
- 2 tablespoons of warm water
- food colour
- writing icing

- candles and holders
- decorations

Equipment

- a large mixing bowl
- 3 other bowls
- a cup to break the eggs into
- a sieve
- a teaspoon and a tablespoon
- a wooden spoon
- scales or a balance
- greaseproof paper
- 2 round baking tins

Safety Advice on Using Eggs
(page 7)

What you do

1. Weigh the eggs, then measure out the same weight of butter, sugar and flour. Put each in a separate bowl.
2. Line the base of the tins with greaseproof paper (to stop the cake sticking).
3. Set the oven at 180°C (350°F), gas mark 4.
4. Cream the butter and sugar with the wooden spoon in the big bowl until it is soft and fluffy.
5. Break the eggs into the cup one at a time and add to the mixture, stirring all the time. Each time you add an egg, add a tablespoon of flour.
6. Add the remaining flour and the vanilla flavouring.
7. The mixture should be a soft 'dropping' consistency. If it is too dry, add a little milk or water.
8. Spoon the mixture into the two tins, sharing it evenly. Smooth the surface with a knife or spatula.
9. Bake for 25 to 30 minutes, until golden brown. Test if it's cooked by gently pushing a knife into the cake. If it comes out clean, the cake is cooked.
10. Remove from the oven and allow to cool a bit before turning out onto the wire rack. Don't ice it until it is completely cold.
11. Sieve the icing sugar and add the water a little at a time.
12. Colour with food colouring, write messages and add decorations.

Other activities

- ▶ Make birthday cards.
- ▶ Print wrapping paper and cards.
- ▶ Have a birthday party in the garden (any birthday is a good excuse for a celebration!).
- ▶ Set up a post office for letters and parcels.
- ▶ Have a concert at the party.

Early Learning Goals

PSD Be interested, excited and motivated to learn.
Have a developing respect for their own cultures and beliefs, and those of other people.

LCC Interact with others, negotiating plans and activities.

PSRN Say and use number names in order in familiar contexts.
Count reliably up to ten everyday objects.
Recognise numerals 1–9.

CR Explore colour, texture and shape, in two and three dimension.

Story: Making Faces

Recipe: Expression Biscuits

This book will encourage looking at expressions. Use a mirror to help the children to look at their own faces, and see if they can reproduce them in icing.

What you need for face biscuits:

You could make your own biscuits, or concentrate on making faces and use ready-made biscuits.

Ingredients

▶ packets of round biscuits (e.g. Digestive and Rich Tea)

▶ icing made from 225g (8oz) icing sugar and 2 tablespoons of water

▶ food colouring

▶ gravy browning

For the icing

▶ sprinkles, small jellies and halved cherries

Equipment

▶ small bowls for different colours of icing

▶ saucers or egg cups for food colouring

▶ butter knives for spreading icing

▶ a wooden spoon

▶ scales

▶ a wire cooling rack

▶ mirrors

▶ cotton buds

What you do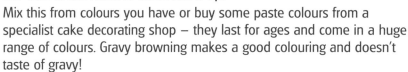

1. Make the biscuits or unwrap the packets.
2. Make some skin coloured icing. The colours should not be too dark or the features won't show up.

   Mix this from colours you have or buy some paste colours from a specialist cake decorating shop – they last for ages and come in a huge range of colours. Gravy browning makes a good colouring and doesn't taste of gravy!
3. Talk about skin/eye/hair colour with the children.
4. Put different colours of icing in different bowls.
5. Ice the biscuits with chosen colours. Each child could do several biscuits.
6. Put the biscuits on the wire racks and leave somewhere warm to dry. If you do the next bit too soon, the colours will run!
7. Put a few drops of blue, red, green and brown colouring in saucers or egg cups and add a few drops of water.
8. Set up mirrors where the children can see themselves as they work.
9. When the first layer of icing is dry, use the cotton buds and other decorations to make expressions on the biscuits.
10. Talk about expressions and features as the children work.

   * Leave to dry before eating.

Other activities

▶ Make some expressions masks by cutting photos from magazines and mounting them on card. Add a stick and use to play games.

▶ Play the expressions game – one child makes a face, the other guesses what they are feeling.

▶ Put mirrors in role-play areas, outside, on the ground and on doors.

Early Learning Goals

PSD Have a developing respect for their own cultures and beliefs, and those of others.

LCC Use talk to organise, sequence and clarify thinking, ideas, feelings and events.

K&U Investigate objects and materials by using all of their senses.

Find out about and identify some features of living things.

Look closely at similarities and differences.

CR Use their imagination in art.

Story: Sally and the Limpet

Recipe: Deep Sea Jellies

**Read about Sally's adventure with a limpet that wouldn't let go.
Then make some seaside jellies.**

What you need for a 600ml (1 pint) jelly:

Ingredients

- 3 tablespoons of hot water

- 1 sachet (1 tablespoon) of gelatin

- 600ml (1 pint) clear apple juice

- a few drops of blue and green food colouring

- jelly fish, worms and liquorice strands sweets

Equipment

- a large bowl

- a tablespoon

- clear cups, individual jelly moulds or a big jelly mould

If you haven't got a jelly mould, use a bowl or plastic box. For all these jelly recipes, you can use a packet jelly instead of gelatin.

What you do

1. Put the hot water in the bowl and sprinkle the gelatin on top.
2. Stir until the gelatin has fully melted.
3. Add the apple juice and a few drops of colouring (a mixture of blue and green will make a suitable sea colour).
4. Pour half the jelly into the jelly mould(s) and leave it to set for a while.
5. When the jelly is beginning to really set, add the jelly fish, worms and liquorice strands for seaweed. Then add the rest of the jelly.
6. Leave to set completely, then tip out onto a plate or serve from the mould.

Some more ideas for jelly

▶ You can also use the above method to make Halloween jellies, with jelly bugs and spiders in blackcurrant jelly.

▶ Or make jelly shapes by making a jelly in a shallow pan or baking tray. Leave to set, then use cookie cutters to cut out shapes, letters or numbers. Lift onto plates with a spatula.

▶ Make a jelly sea by colouring a jelly blue or green and whisking with a fork after it has set. Make some paper or cucumber boats to float on the jelly sea.

▶ Try making a milk jelly. Mix the jelly powder or gelatin with a small amount of hot water and top up with milk.

Other activities

▶ Mix food colouring or Edicol in the water tray for a change.

▶ Make a seaside in the sand tray with shells, stones, plastic crabs and starfish.

▶ Make a sandy beach in a cement mixing tray outside. Walk through the sand with bare feet!

Early Learning Goals

PSD	Select and use activities and resources independently.	Ask questions about why things happen and how things work.
LCC	Respond to stories.	**PH**
PSRN	Count reliably up to ten everyday objects.	Handle tools, objects, construction and malleable materials with increasing control.
	Recognise numerals 1–10.	**CR**
K&U	Look closely at change.	Explore colour, texture, shape, form and space.

Story: Having a Picnic

Recipe: Currant Buns

Make traditional currant buns and act out this simple family story with a picnic basket and a blanket.

What you need for 16 buns:

Ingredients
- ▶ 500g (1lb) white bread flour
- ▶ 1 sachet of easy blend dried yeast
- ▶ 85g (3oz) sugar
- ▶ ¼ teaspoon of salt
- ▶ 250ml (½ pint) milk or milk and water
- ▶ ½ teaspoon of ground cinnamon
- ▶ 112g (4oz) currants
- ▶ 30g (1oz) dried mixed peel
- ▶ 85g (3oz) butter
- ▶ 2 eggs
- ▶ milk and sugar to glaze

Equipment
- ▶ a large mixing bowl
- ▶ a sieve
- ▶ a teaspoon
- ▶ a tablespoon
- ▶ a wooden spoon
- ▶ cling film
- ▶ a measuring jug and scales
- ▶ a pastry brush
- ▶ baking trays and a wire rack

What you do

1. Weigh the flour and sieve into the large bowl.
2. Add the salt and dried yeast, sugar, currants, peel and spice.
3. Melt the butter in the microwave or over hot water and add to the mixture.
4. Break the eggs into a cup and add to the mixture.
5. Gradually mix in the milk or milk and water with the wooden spoon until the dough is well mixed.
6. Cover the mixing bowl with an oiled piece of cling film.
7. Leave the dough in a warm place for at least an hour until it has doubled in size and feels spongy. (The cling film allows you and the children to see what is happening!)
8. Uncover the bowl and take small pieces to shape into round buns. (Putting some flour on the children's hands will stop the dough sticking.)
9. Put the buns on a greased baking tray, leaving space between for the buns to spread.
10. Put the trays in a warm place for 20 minutes to rise again.
11. Heat the oven to 230°C (450°F), gas mark 8.
12. Bake the buns for 15 minutes. If you want them to be shiny on top, take them out of the oven just before they are finished and brush the tops with a mixture of milk and sugar. Return to the oven to finish cooking. Cool before eating.

Other activities

▶ You can make these buns into hot cross buns by cutting a cross in the top with a sharp knife before baking them.
▶ Sing 'Five Brown Buns'.
▶ Have a picnic in your garden or the park.
▶ Retell the story in the hall or the garden.

Early Learning Goals

LCC Use talk to organise, sequence and clarify thinking, ideas, feelings and events.
Retell narratives in the correct sequence drawing on the language patterns of stories.

PSRN Use language such as 'heavier' or 'lighter'.

K&U Look closely at change.
Ask questions about why things happen.

PH Recognise the importance of keeping healthy and things that contribute to this.

Story: The Little Boat

Recipe: Sailing Boat Rolls

Read this story about a boy and his adventurous boat, then make little edible boats to sail on a lettuce sea.

What you need for 16 little boats:

Ingredients

- a packet of 8 'bridge' type rolls
- butter or margarine
- fillings – chopped hard boiled egg, mashed tuna, grated cheese or anything else you fancy
- coloured paper for the sails
- cocktail sticks

> **Safety Advice on Using Eggs (page 7)**

- a lettuce for the sea (iceberg lettuce works best)

Equipment

- chopping boards
- butter knives
- spoons
- small bowls for fillings
- scissors
- a large plate or tray for serving

I will need

What you do

1. Cut some triangles from coloured paper for sails.
2. Thread each sail onto a cocktail stick.
3. Help the children to prepare the fillings and put them in bowls with spoons. Stir a spoonful of mayonnaise or plain yogurt into the fillings to make them easier to manage.
4. Cut the bridge rolls in half lengthways to make two boats from each.
5. Children can spread their own butter/margarine and select their own fillings.
6. When they are happy with their boat, let them add a sail.
7. Float the boats on a sea of shredded lettuce.

You don't need a cooker for cookery! Sandwich making and other cold cookery are excellent ways of developing skills of:

▶ fine motor control
▶ making choices
▶ working independently
▶ sharing a task

and offering enjoyable experiences such as:

▶ discussing flavours and smells
▶ enjoying making things for others
▶ enjoying sharing food
▶ discussing changes and differences.

Other activities

▶ Use the water tray to explore floating and sinking.
▶ Make boats with small offcuts of wood, garden stick masts and sails cut from carrier bag plastic.
▶ Explore how water behaves with a water construction set such as Aqualab.
▶ Sing songs about the sea.

Early Learning Goals

PSD Work as part of a group or class, taking turns and sharing fairly.

LCC Interact with others, negotiating plans and activities and taking turns.

PSRN Say and use number names in order in familiar contexts. Count reliably to ten. Recognise numerals 1–9.

K&U Select tools and techniques they need to shape, assemble and join the materials they are using.

Story: When the Teddy Bears Came

Recipe: Honey Buns

Help children to manage a new arrival by sharing this story, where a new baby triggers a torrent of bears!

What you need for 12 honey buns:

I will need

Ingredients

▶ 225g (8oz) self-raising flour
▶ a pinch of salt
▶ 1 level teaspoon of bicarbonate of soda
▶ 2 teaspoons of cream of tartar
▶ 2 teaspoons of mixed spice
▶ 100g (3oz) butter/margarine
▶ 60g (2oz) sugar

Equipment

▶ scales
▶ a sieve
▶ a large mixing bowl
▶ a teaspoon
▶ a tablespoon
▶ a small bowl
▶ patty tins
▶ a wire cooling rack

What you do

Children can do the whole of this recipe to step 10 with little or no help. They just need a supportive adult to talk them through the process.

1. Heat the oven to 220°C (425°F), gas mark 7.
2. Weigh the flour and sieve it into the bowl.
3. Add the salt, bicarbonate of soda, cream of tartar and spice.
4. Add the butter or margarine and rub it in with your fingers until it looks like fine breadcrumbs.
5. Add the sugar.
6. Warm the honey jar a bit to make it easier to measure (put it on a radiator or in a microwave for a few seconds).
7. Add the honey and a little milk.
8. Mix with a wooden spoon to make a soft, spooning dough.
9. Grease the patty tins.
10. Spoon the mixture into the tins.
11. Bake for 15 to 20 minutes until well risen and golden brown.
12. Lift onto a wire rack to cool.

You could make these buns with golden syrup or black treacle (molasses) for a change. Just replace the honey with one or the other.

Other activities

► Make bees and explore hexagons.
► Have a teddy bears' picnic.
► Use the construction sets to make houses or caves for bears.
► Turn your role-play area into the Three Bears Cafe. Make furry ears and furry gloves in three sizes for the customers to wear. Make sure the menu includes porridge!

Early Learning Goals

PSD Continue to be interested, excited and motivated to learn.

LCC Use talk to organise, sequence and clarify thinking, ideas, feelings and events.

PSRN Say and use number names in order in familiar contexts. Count reliably to ten.

K&U Find out about and identify features of living things.

CR Respond in a variety of ways to what they see, hear, smell, touch and feel.

Story: Don't Forget the Bacon!

Recipe: Bacon Sandwiches

Read this favourite rhyming story, then make some bacon sandwiches. If bacon is an unsuitable filling in your setting, you could use cheese.

What you need for bacon sandwiches:

Ingredients

▶ sliced bread (white or brown), one slice per child

▶ bacon rashers (2 per sandwich) – streaky bacon is very suitable

▶ tomato sauce (optional)

▶ butter or margarine

▶ a small amount of oil if you are frying the bacon

Equipment

▶ chopping boards

▶ butter knives or other blunt knives

▶ an adult knife

▶ a frying pan or grill pan

▶ a spatula or fork for turning

▶ plates

Remember that active young children need the energy from fats, even though adults might not!

What you do

1. Help the children to spread their own bread with butter or margarine.
2. Cut each slice in half.
3. Oil the frying pan and heat it up (adult only).
4. Fry the bacon until crispy.
5. Talk to the children about what is happening – how the bacon changes as it cooks and the smell of the bacon cooking. If possible, sit the children safely so they can see the frying pan or grill.
6. When the bacon is cooked, put two rashers on one half of each sandwich.
7. Top with tomato sauce (optional).
8. Put the other half of the bread on top.
9. Cut the sandwich in two.
10. Eat and enjoy!

Spreading and making sandwiches is a simple activity which children love. It gives them a range of opportunities to learn independently, use tools safely, select ingredients and make food to share.

Some alternative sandwiches are:
- cream cracker biscuits with butter and grated or cream cheese
- Ryvita with Marmite as an open sandwich
- peanut butter (check for allergies first)
- bread, butter and sliced tomato, cucumber or grated carrot.

Other activities

▶ Make sandwiches and have a picnic.
▶ Read 'The Giant Jam Sandwich'.
▶ Have a parents and carers party. Make your own rolls and spread them with a range of fillings.
▶ Make butter from full fat milk. Put the milk in a screw-top jar and shake until the butter appears.

Early Learning Goals

PSD	Continue to be interested, excited and motivated to learn.		need to shape, assemble and join materials.
LCC	Respond to stories. Use talk to organise, sequence and clarify thinking.	**PH**	Handle tools and objects safely and with increasing control.
K&U	Select tools and techniques they	**CR**	Respond in a variety of ways to what they smell, touch and feel.

Story: Dogger

Recipe: Chocolate Pennies

A favourite bedtime toy ends up on sale at a school fête with a price on its head! Make some chocolate pennies to eat as they listen to the story.

What you need for 30 small cookies:

Ingredients

This easy recipe is all in spoonfuls.

- ▶ 8 tablespoons of soft brown sugar
- ▶ 1 egg
- ▶ 5 tablespoons and 1 teaspoon of cooking oil
- ▶ 2 tablespoons of cocoa powder
- ▶ 16 tablespoons of self-raising flour
- ▶ 5 tablespoons of chocolate chips
- ▶ 5 tablespoons of chopped white chocolate

Equipment

- ▶ a large mixing bowl
- ▶ a sieve
- ▶ a teaspoon
- ▶ a tablespoon
- ▶ a fork
- ▶ a cup to break the egg into
- ▶ baking trays
- ▶ a wire cooling rack and a spatula

Safety Advice on Using Eggs (page 7)

What you do

1. Heat the oven to 180°C (350°F), gas mark 4.
2. Chop the white chocolate.
3. Put the sugar and oil in the bowl.
4. Break the egg into the cup and pour into the bowl.
5. Mix well with a fork.
6. Put the sieve over the bowl and spoon in the flour and the cocoa powder.
7. Shake the sieve gently to sieve the flour and cocoa powder.
8. Mix gently.
9. Add the two sorts of chocolate and mix again.
10. Knead lightly with your hands to make a soft dough.
11. Spoon out pieces of dough with the teaspoon and shape into balls with your hands. This will make little cookies.
12. Put the balls on a greased baking tray at least 2cm apart because they spread when they cook.
13. Bake for 10 to 12 minutes at 180°C (350°F), gas mark 4 (watch carefully; these little cookies will cook quickly).
14. Remove from the oven and cool on a wire rack.

This recipe is easy enough for even the youngest children to do stages 2 to 12 on their own with 'arms' length' guidance from an adult.

Other activities

▶ Use the cookies for counting.
▶ Set up a role-play sale with old or new toys. Children can make the labels and signs. Use real money for shopping.
▶ Talk about favourite bedtime toys and perhaps bring them to school.
▶ Play 'expressions' as you read the story again.

Early Learning Goals

PSD Work as part of a group.

LCC Listen with enjoyment and respond to stories.
Retell narratives in the correct sequences, drawing on the language patterns of stories.

K&U Investigate objects and materials by using all their senses.

PH Handle tools, objects and malleable materials safely and with increasing control.

CR Respond to what they see, smell, touch and feel.

Story: It's the Bear!

Recipe: Baby Blueberry Muffins

A new slant on the bear in the woods. Mum is at last convinced that the bear is real!

What you need for 16 small muffins:

Ingredients

This easy recipe is all in spoonfuls.

- ▶ 220g (8oz) self-raising flour
- ▶ 50g (2oz) soft brown sugar
- ▶ 110g (4oz) blueberries (fresh or frozen)
- ▶ 1 egg
- ▶ 250ml (1 cup) milk
- ▶ 2 tablespoons of cooking oil
- ▶ paper baking cases

> **Safety Advice on Using Eggs (page 7)**

Equipment

- ▶ a large mixing bowl
- ▶ a sieve
- ▶ a teaspoon and a fork
- ▶ a tablespoon
- ▶ a wooden spoon
- ▶ measuring jug and scales
- ▶ a small bowl to mix the egg and milk
- ▶ muffin or bun tins
- ▶ a wire cooling rack

If you can get really small baking cases, you can make lots of tiny muffins.

What you do

These muffins are best eaten while they are still warm.

1. Heat the oven to 190°C (375°F), gas mark 5.
2. Put the cake cases in the muffin or bun tins.
3. Weigh the flour and sieve it into the mixing bowl.
4. Mix in the sugar.
5. Break the egg into the small bowl and mix it with the fork.
6. Add the milk and oil to the egg in the small bowl.
7. Add the frozen blueberries to this mixture.
8. Now add the blueberry, eggy, milky mixture to the flour in the big bowl.
9. Stir gently until just mixed (don't stir too much – it doesn't matter if you can still see some flour).
10. Spoon the mixture into the cake cases and put straight in the oven.
11. Bake for 12 to 15 minutes until well risen and brown. If you use very small cake cases, the muffins will cook more quickly.
12. Cool on the wire rack and eat while still warm.

* If you use frozen blueberries, don't thaw them first – mix them in frozen.
* You can use this recipe for chocolate chip, raisin or banana muffins. Just substitute 50g (2oz) of chocolate chips, raisins or one small ripe banana for the blueberries.

Other activities

▶ Sing 'The Muffin Man'.
▶ Try some more unfamiliar fruits.
▶ Make some fake muffins with flour and salt dough, bake and use in role play.
▶ Visit a baker's shop and look at all the different sorts of bread and muffins.

Early Learning Goals

PSD Select and use activities and resources independently.

LCC Show an understanding of elements of stories, such as main characte and sequence of events.

K&U Investigate objects and materials by using all of their senses.

CR Use their imagination in art and design, imaginative role play and stories.

Story: Rosie's Walk

Recipe: Popcorn Strings

Use this popular story to sequence and predict as Rosie walks through the farmyard, unaware of the following fox. This story is perfect for dramatising!

What you need for 2 lots of popcorn strings:

Ingredients

▶ 2 tablespoons of cooking oil

▶ 220g (8oz) popcorn kernels (try a health food store if you have difficulty finding it)

▶ darning needles

▶ wool or coloured thread

Equipment

▶ a large saucepan with a tight-fitting lid

▶ a large bowl

▶ a tablespoon

▶ food colouring

▶ ziplock plastic bags

What you do

1. Talk to the children about popcorn and explain what you are going to do.
2. Look carefully at some of the corn kernels. Talk about them.
3. Put 2 tablespoons of the oil in the saucepan and heat over a high heat.
4. When the oil is hot, add half the corn and put on the lid.
5. Gently shake the pan to cover the corn with oil.
6. As the corn begins to pop, keep shaking the pan to prevent burning.
7. The popcorn is ready when the popping stops.
8. Tip the popcorn into the big bowl and leave to cool.
9. 'Pop' the rest of the corn.
10. When all the corn is cool, thread some needles with coloured thread or wool.
11. Show the children how to thread the popcorn on the thread to make necklaces, bracelets or decorations.
12. If you want coloured popcorn, pour some popped corn in a plastic ziplock bag with just a drop or two of food colouring.
13. Fasten the bag and shake gently to colour the corn.

Birds love these popcorn strings, so make sure you make enough to put some in the garden for them.

Other activities

▶ Use the strings to decorate an outside Christmas tree for the birds. Add some strings of peanuts in their shells (check for allergies first). Make some bird cake. Hang apples on strings from trees and bushes.

▶ Make some sequencing pictures of 'Rosie's Walk'.

▶ Chalk Rosie's walk on the ground.

Early Learning Goals

PSD	Continue to be excited and motivated to learn. Be confident to try new activities.	
K&U	Find out about and identify some features of objects and events they observe.	
PH	Use a range of small and large	

equipment.
Handle tools and objects safely.

CR Explore texture, shape and form in two and three dimensions.
Respond in a variety of ways to what they see, hear, smell, touch and feel.

Story: Hello Beaky

Recipe: Meringue Nests

Beaky searches for his mother. Use his story to talk about eggs, babies, families and feelings. Then make some nests.

What you need for 24 meringue nests:

I will need

Ingredients

▶ 6 egg whites (use the yolks to make scrambled egg), or buy egg whites from a supermarket

▶ 350g (12oz) caster sugar

▶ a pinch of salt

▶ sugar or chocolate mini eggs

> Salmonella is a health risk for young children. Get guaranteed salmonella-free eggs or buy pasteurised egg whites from a supermarket.

Equipment

▶ a large mixing bowl

▶ a small bowl

▶ 2 cups to separate the eggs into

▶ baking parchment

▶ baking trays

▶ a hand or electric whisk

▶ a tablespoon or knife

▶ scales

▶ a wire cooling rack

What you do

Making meringues is very simple – you just need to be sure that the equipment you use is absolutely clean and that not one spot of egg yolk gets into the whites. Meringues don't work if they have any fat in them.

1. Put sheets of baking parchment on the baking trays.
2. Crack each egg very gently and separate the white from the yolk. (Tap each egg on the edge of the bowl to break the shell, then tip the yolk from one half of the egg shell to the other so the white slips into the cup. Put each yolk into the other cup and pour the white into the big bowl.)
3. Continue until all the eggs are separated.
4. Add the salt to the egg whites and whisk them until they become stiff. An electric whisk will do this quicker, but it's not so much fun. The mixture should stand up in a peak when you lift the whisk out of the bowl.
5. Spoon half the sugar into the egg white and whisk again.
6. Take the whisk out and add the other half of the sugar. Fold the sugar gently into the mixture with a metal tablespoon or a knife.
7. Spoon tablespoonfuls of the mixture onto the baking sheets and gently make a hollow in each nest with the back of the spoon.
8. Bake at 110°C (225°F), gas mark 1/4 for about 3 hours, until the meringues are firm and come away from the parchment easily. When cool, fill with chocolate eggs.

Other activities

▶ Look at different sorts of eggs.
▶ Find other books about mothers and babies.
▶ Retell Beaky's adventures in the sand tray or on a play mat with plastic animals.
▶ Make animal masks or use finger puppets to retell the story.

Early Learning Goals

LCC Use talk to organise, sequence and clarify thinking, ideas, feelings and events.

PSRN Say and use number names in order in familiar contexts. Countreliably up to ten objects.

K&U Find out about and identify some features of living things and events they observe.

PH Use a range of small equipment and handle tools safely.

CR Explore colour, texture and shape.

Story: Lights for Gita

Recipe: Chapattis

Use this story or another favourite Asian tale – then get their hands busy with some chapattis.

What you need for 20 small chapattis:

Ingredients

▶ 175g (6oz) white plain flour – plus 50g (2oz) extra

▶ 175g (6oz) wholemeal flour

▶ 1 teaspoon of salt

▶ 1 tablespoon of ghee or melted butter (Ghee is clarified butter – you can get it in tins at Asian grocers.)

▶ 180ml (¾ cup) warm water

Equipment

▶ a large mixing bowl

▶ a teaspoon

▶ a tablespoon

▶ a wooden spoon

▶ pastry boards and rolling pins

▶ cling film

▶ a measuring jug

▶ scales

▶ a heavy frying pan

▶ a plate

▶ a wire cooling rack

What you do

1. Put the flours into the big bowl.
2. Add the salt.
3. Rub in the ghee or melted butter with your fingertips.
4. Add enough water to make a firm dough.
5. Knead the dough on a floured board or clean worktop, working in the extra 50g of flour.
6. Put the dough back in the bowl, cover with cling film and leave to stand for 1 hour.
7. Divide the dough into 20 pieces.
8. Roll each piece out on a floured board into a 12 to 15cm round shape.
9. Put the chapattis on a plate and cover with a cloth or cling film.
10. Heat the frying pan until very hot (no oil or butter).
11. Cook the chapattis one at a time on one side until they have little brown spots all over. Turn them over and cook on the other side.
12. Wrap the chapattis in a cloth to keep them warm while you cook the rest.

* Eat the chapattis as they are or with butter.

** Or you could make some cucumber and yogurt raita. Chop a cucumber into small pieces and mix with plain yogurt and a tiny pinch of cayenne pepper.

Other activities

▶ Visit an Indian grocers.
▶ Make Diwali lamps (divas) from clay or salt dough.
▶ Try smelling different spices and herbs.
▶ Make rangoli patterns.
▶ Have a Diwali party. Invite parents to share Asian food.

Early Learning Goals

PSD Have a developing respect for their own cultures and beliefs, and those of other people.

LCC Use talk to organise, sequence and clarify thinking, ideas, feelings and events. Retell narratives.

K&U Investigate objects and materials by using all of their senses.

CR Respond to what they see, hear, smell, touch and feel.

Story: The Last Noo-noo

Recipe: Monster Cheese Biscuits

Most children will understand this story about a monster who finds it difficult to part with his dummy.

What you need for 16 monster biscuits:

Ingredients

▶ 220g (8oz) plain flour
▶ 110g (4oz) butter or margarine
▶ 175g (6oz) grated cheese
▶ a pinch of salt
▶ a pinch of cayenne pepper
▶ 1 egg

> **Safety Advice on Using Eggs (page 7)**

Equipment

▶ a large mixing bowl
▶ a sieve
▶ a teaspoon
▶ a tablespoon
▶ a wooden spoon
▶ scales
▶ a cheese grater
▶ a board and rolling pins
▶ butter knives
▶ monster shapes or cutters
▶ a spatula
▶ baking trays and a wire rack

What you do

1. Grate the cheese.
2. Use the template at the end of the book (page 64) to make your own monster shape.
3. Preheat the oven to 200°C (400°F), gas mark 6.
4. Sieve the flour into the bowl.
5. Add the butter or margarine and rub in with your fingers until the mixture looks like fine breadcrumbs.
6. Stir in the grated cheese, the salt and the cayenne pepper.
7. Add the egg and mix with fingers until the mixture sticks together (if it is too dry, add a little water).
8. Share out the dough and roll out on boards or a clean work surface.
9. Cut out monsters from the dough with cutters or card shapes.
10. Re-roll the dough to make more biscuits.
11. When you get to the last few bits, make cheese straws or little rounds by making balls and flattening them.
12. Lift the monsters onto the baking tray with the spatula.
13. Bake for 10–15 minutes until golden brown.
14. Cool on the wire tray before eating.

* For added flavour, try sprinkling a little grated Parmesan on the biscuits before cooking.

Other activities

▶ Make monster masks and act out the story.
▶ Talk about growing up and giving up favourite toys etc.
▶ Make your own 'baby' tree, hung with all the things babies like.
▶ Invite a mother or father or baby to school.
▶ Make a role-play baby clinic.

Early Learning Goals

PSD Be confident to try new activities, initiate ideas and speak in a familiar group.

LCC Use talk to organise, sequence and clarify thinking, ideas, feelings and events.

PSRN Say and use number names in order in familiar contexts.

K&U Investigate objects and materials by using all of their senses.

CR Respond in a variety of ways to what they see, hear, smell, touch and feel.

Story: The Baked Bean Queen

Recipe: Bean Dip

A popular story about a popular food. The Queen knows exactly what she wants to eat (for every meal). Make a different dish for your baked bean kings and queens.

What you need for bean dip:

Ingredients

► 400g (12oz) tin of cannellini beans (they are white)

► ½ a small onion, chopped

► 1 clove of garlic (optional)

► 1 tablespoon of fresh or bottled lemon juice

► 2 tablespoons of olive oil

► salt and black pepper

► 1 tablespoon of fresh basil, chopped (or 1 teaspoon of dried basil)

► 1 tablespoon of chopped parsley

► corn chips or pitta bread

Equipment

► a large mixing bowl

► a teaspoon and a tablespoon

► a knife

► a food processor, a blender or a potato masher (you could even use a fork)

► a sieve

► a serving bowl

I will need

What you do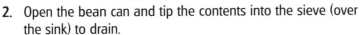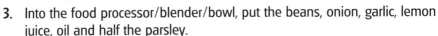

1. Peel the onion and garlic, and chop them finely.
2. Open the bean can and tip the contents into the sieve (over the sink) to drain.
3. Into the food processor/blender/bowl, put the beans, onion, garlic, lemon juice, oil and half the parsley.
4. Season with salt and pepper.
5. If you are using a processor or blender, blend for 30 seconds, scrape the mixture down, then blend for another 30 seconds.
6. If you are using a bowl, mash the dip with a fork or potato masher until it is smooth.
7. Transfer to the serving dish and sprinkle with the rest of the parsley.
8. Warm the pitta bread for a few seconds in a microwave and cut into slices.
9. Dip the pitta (or corn chips) in the dip to eat.
* You can also make the dip with black-eyed beans, red kidney beans, butter beans or even baked beans.
** You can also use the same recipe with tinned chick peas to make simple hummus.
*** Use vegetable sticks (carrot, celery or cucumber) for a change.

Other activities

▶ Look at different sorts of beans. Discuss colour, shape, size, taste and smell.

▶ Get some bean seeds from a garden centre and grow them in jars, tubs or growbags.

▶ Read 'Jack and the Beanstalk' and act it out. Use the climbing frame for a beanstalk.

Early Learning Goals

LCC	Retell narratives in the correct sequence.		Ask questions about why things happen and how things work.
	Show an understanding of elements of stories, such as main character and sequence of events.	**PH**	Recognise the importance of keeping healthy and things that contribute to this.
K&U	Investigate objects and materials by using all of their senses.	**CR**	Respond to what they see, hear, smell, touch and feel.

Story: Meg and Mog

Recipe: Pumpkin Soup

Cook up an autumn spell in your cooking cauldron to sip while you tell the story.

What you need for 16 small servings:

Ingredients

- 1kg (about 2lb) of pumpkin
- 2 medium onions
- 2 tablespoons of butter or margarine
- 4 bacon rashers (optional)
- 3 pints of water
- 2 chicken or vegetable stock cubes
- 1 small carton of cream or plain yogurt
- bread

Equipment

- chopping boards
- knives
- a teaspoon
- tablespoons
- a wooden spoon
- a large saucepan with a lid
- a measuring jug
- scales
- scissors
- a potato masher
- a ladle
- bowls or mugs and spoons

What you do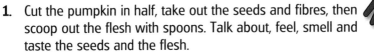

1. Cut the pumpkin in half, take out the seeds and fibres, then scoop out the flesh with spoons. Talk about, feel, smell and taste the seeds and the flesh.
2. Weigh the pumpkin flesh and talk about how much you need.
3. Peel and chop the onions.
4. With the scissors, cut the rind from the bacon and cut the rashers into small pieces.
5. Put the butter in the pan and turn on the heat to medium.
6. When the butter is melted, put in the onion and the bacon.
7. Stir with the wooden spoon until the onion is soft.
8. Add the scooped pumpkin flesh, the water and crumbled stock cubes.
9. Put the lid on the pan and turn the heat to high.
10. When the soup boils, remove the lid and turn the heat to low.
11. Simmer for 30 minutes until the pumpkin is cooked. Try it by poking it with a knife (it should feel just soft).
12. Turn the stove off and leave to cool for 10 minutes.
13. Use the masher to mash the pumpkin until the soup is smooth.
14. Add the cream or yogurt and heat again until it is hot.
15. Ladle into bowls or mugs and eat with slices of bread.
* You could add a pinch of cayenne pepper or cinnamon for extra flavour.

Other activities

▶ Buy another pumpkin and make a Jack-o-Lantern. Cut off the top, hollow out the middle, make eyes, nose and mouth, and put a night light inside.
▶ Save some pumpkin seeds and grow them in pots or growbags.
▶ Wash the seeds, dry them and use them for counting or threading.

Early Learning Goals

PSD Work as part of a class, taking turns and sharing fairly.

LCC Respond to stories, songs, other music, rhymes and poems.

K&U Investigate objects and materials by using all of their senses.

PH Use a range of small equipment. Handle tools and objects safely and with increasing control.

CR Explore colour, texture, shape, form and space in two and three dimensions.

Story: Oliver's Fruit Salad

Recipe: Fruit Ice Lollies

Use some of Oliver's fruit to make frozen fruit-flavoured lollies
– lickalicious!

What you need for 8 lollies:

Ingredients

▶ 450g mango slices (tinned or
   fresh) or 1kg (about 2lb) water
   melon

▶ 100g (4oz) caster sugar

▶ 250ml (1 cup) water

Equipment

▶ a chopping board
▶ a sharp knife
▶ a tablespoon
▶ a sieve (for draining)
▶ a saucepan
▶ a wooden spoon
▶ a measuring jug
▶ ice lolly moulds
▶ ice lolly sticks

What you do

You can make the syrup beforehand and leave it to cool before making the lollies.

1. Make the sugar syrup by mixing the sugar and water in a saucepan and stirring over a medium heat until the sugar is dissolved and the syrup looks clear.

2. Reduce the heat and simmer the syrup without stirring for 8 minutes. Turn off the heat and measure the liquid. You should have about half a cup (125ml). If you have more, boil for a bit longer. If you have less, top up with water.

3. Wash, peel and chop the mango or melon (if you are using tinned mango, open the tin and drain the fruit in the strainer).

4. Put the fruit in a bowl and mash it with the potato masher.

5. Add the sugar syrup and stir until well mixed.

6. Carefully pour the mixture into the moulds and put the lollies in the freezer compartment of a fridge for an hour or until the ice begins to set.

7. Push a stick into each lolly and return to the freezer over night or until fully set.

* If you haven't got lolly moulds, freeze the mixture in ice cube trays, egg cups or small plastic containers.

Other activities

▶ Explore other liquids as they freeze and melt.

▶ Make some big blocks of ice in plastic boxes and float them in the water tray. Watch as they melt.

▶ Make ice with food colouring in and see what happens as it freezes.

▶ Freeze tiny objects (sequins, beads, berries and pebbles) in ice cubes.

Early Learning Goals

PSD	Continue to be interested, excited and motivated to learn.
K&U	Investigate objects by using all of their senses. Look closely at differences and change. Ask questions about why things happen.

PH	Recognise the importance of keeping healthy and things that contribute to this.
CR	Explore colour, shape and form. Respond in a variety of ways to what they see, hear, smell, touch and feel.

Templates

Template – Elmer the Elephant (pages 30–31)

Template – Monster Biscuits (pages 56–57)

Book List

Title	Author	Publisher
The Three Bears	Traditional	Ladybird
The Big Pancake	Traditional	Ladybird
The Enormous Turnip	Elizabeth Laird	Picture Mammoth
The Gingerbread Man	Mary Hoffman	Macmillan
The Little Red Hen	Traditional	Ladybird
The Very Hungry Caterpillar	Eric Carle	Hamish Hamilton
Oliver's Milkshake	Vivian French	Hodder
Handa's Surprise	Eileen Browne	Walker Books
Pass the Jam, Jim	Kaye Umansky	Red Fox
Pete's a Pizza	William Steig	Red Fox
Elmer the Elephant	David McKee	Red Fox
Danny's Birthday	Mike Dickinson	Scholastic
Making Faces	Nick Butterworth	Walker Books
Sally and the Limpet	Simon James	Walker Books
Having a Picnic	Sarah Garland	Picture Puffin
The Little Boat	Kathy Henderson	Walker Books
When the Teddy Bears Came	Martin Waddell	Walker Books
Don't Forget the Bacon!	Pat Hutchins	Picture Puffin
Dogger	Shirley Hughes	Red Fox
It's the Bear!	Jez Alborough	Walker Books
Rosie's Walk	Pat Hutchins	Penguin
Hello Beaky	Jez Alborough	Walker Books
Lights for Gita	Rachma Gilmore	Second Story
The Last Noo-noo	Jill Murphy	Walker Books
The Baked Bean Queen	Rose Impey	Picture Puffin
Meg and Mog	Helen Nicoll	Picture Puffin
Oliver's Fruit Salad	Vivian French	Hodder

More Conversions

One cup of:	is equal to grams	ounces
flour	150g	6oz
butter/block margarine	225g	8oz
icing sugar	125g	5oz
castor sugar	225g	8oz
yogurt	250g	9oz
grated cheese	100g	4oz
porridge oats	100g	4oz
molasses/golden syrup	325g	12oz

Generally

> 1oz = 25 grams (It's actually 28 grams and some books con-
> vert with 25g, some 30g. As long as you keep it standard
> throughout the recipe, this should not be a problem.)
> 16oz = 1 pound
> 2.2lb = 1kg

Liquids (milk, water etc.)

> 1 cup = 250ml = 8 fl oz = 1/2 pint

Our thanks to Mrs S J Shillito of Great Binfields Primary School for contacting us when she found some anomalies in the conversion tables in this book. These have now been corrected.

Notes and Your Own Recipes

I will need

Continuity and progression

The **Baby & Beyond**™ series takes simple activities or resources and shows how they can be used with children at each of the EYFS development stages, from birth to 60+ months. Each double page spread covers one activity, so you can see the progression at a glance.

Shows how simple resources can be used by children at different ages and stages

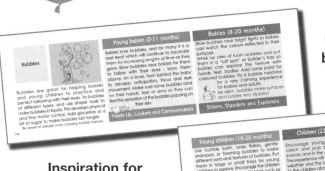

Inspiration for planning continuous provision

Messy Play	978-1-905019-58-8
The Natural World	978-1-905019-57-1
The Sensory World	978-1-905019-60-1
Sound and Music	978-1-905019-59-5
Mark Making	978-1-905019-78-6
Construction	978-1-905019-77-9
Dolls & Soft Toys	978-1-905019-80-9
Bikes, Prams, Pushchairs	978-1-905019-76-2
Role Play	978-1-906029-02-9
Finger Play & Rhymes	978-1-906029-01-2
Dens & Shelters	978-1-906029-03-6
Food	978-1-906029-04-3

through the EYFS

Ideal to support progression and extend learning.

If you have found this book useful you might also like ...

LB Discovery Bottles
ISBN 978-1-9060-2971-5

LB Christmas
ISBN 978-1-9022-3364-2

LB Making Poetry
ISBN 978-1-4081-1250-2

LB Music
ISBN 978-1-9041-8754-7

All available from
www.acblack.com/featherstone/

The Little Books Club

There is always something in Little Books to help and inspire you. Packed full of lovely ideas, Little Books meet the need for exciting and practical activities that are fun to do, address the Early Learning Goals and can be followed in most settings. Everyone is a winner!

We publish 5 new Little Books a year. Little Books Club members receive each of these 5 books as soon as they are published for a reduced price. The subscription cost is £37.50 – a one off payment that buys the 5 new books for £7.50 instead of £8.99 each.

In addition to this, Little Books Club Members receive:
· Free postage and packing on anything ordered from the Featherstone catalogue
· A 15% discount voucher upon joining which can be used to buy any number of books from the Featherstone catalogue
· Members price of £7.50 on any additional Little Book purchased
· A regular, free newsletter dealing with club news, special offers and aspects of Early Years curriculum and practice
· All new Little Books on approval - return in good condition within 30 days and we'll refund the cost to your club account

Call 020 7440 2446 or email: littlebooks@acblack.com for an enrolment pack. Or download an application form from our website:

www.acblack.com/featherstone

The **Little Books** series consists of:

All Through the Year

Bags, Boxes & Trays

Bricks and Boxes

Celebrations

Christmas

Circle Time

Clay and Malleable Materials

Clothes and Fabrics

Colour, Shape and Number

Cooking from Stories

Cooking Together

Counting

Dance

Dance, with music CD

Discovery Bottles

Dough

50

Fine Motor Skills

Fun on a Shoestring

Games with Sounds

Growing Things

ICT

Investigations

Junk Music

Language Fun

Light and Shadow

Listening

Living Things

Look and Listen

Making Books and Cards

Making Poetry

Mark Making

Maths Activities

Maths from Stories

Maths Songs and Games

Messy Play

Music

Nursery Rhymes

Outdoor Play

Outside in All Weathers

Parachute Play

Persona Dolls

Phonics

Playground Games

Prop Boxes for Role Play

Props for Writing

Puppet Making

Puppets in Stories

Resistant Materials

Role Play

Sand and Water

Science through Art

Scissor Skills

Sewing and Weaving

Small World Play

Sound Ideas

Storyboards

Storytelling

Seasons

Time and Money

Time and Place

Treasure Baskets

Treasureboxes

Tuff Spot Activities

Washing Lines

Writing

All available from

www.acblack.com/featherstone